Robin Bright

Designing a Teaching English as a Foreign Language (TEFL) Syllabus

Robin Bright

Designing a Teaching English as a Foreign Language (TEFL) Syllabus

The TEFL Insider

JustFiction Edition

Publisher:
JustFiction! Edition
is a trademark of
International Book Market Service Ltd., member of OmniScriptum Publishing Group
17 Meldrum Street, Beau Bassin 71504, Mauritius
Printed at: see last page
ISBN: 978-620-0-49559-4

Designing a Teaching English as a Foreign Language (TEFL) Syllabus

by Robin Bright

Contents:

Introduction

A multi-dimensional syllabus will be the subject. After a description of the target group for whom the syllabus will be written, that is, language background, level, and institutional context, aims will be discussed. These will derive from a needs analysis of students` perceived needs for a general English course, that is, in terms of language tasks/functions. The context will be presented through a review of the types of syllabi that a multi-dimensional approach seeks to incorporate, that is, the topics, themes, skills, concepts, and/or functions different syllabi apply, but which elements are adaptable to a multi-approach. The course`s subdivision will be in accordance with the 10 week program and the 10 Units in the *Unlock* 1 Reading and Writing by Sabina Ostrowska, and the *Unlock* 1 Listening and Speaking by N. M. White course books. Sequencing will be from Unit 1-10 over the 10 weeks. Before the conclusion, there`ll be an examination of the methodology and rationale for the teaching of the beginner level students and the learning methods applied.

A Cambridge English Placement Test

(http://www.democpt.cambridgetest.org/cptApp/demoTest.html?method
=languageSelection) will be administered and conducted online. The
students will begin at level A1. Using the *Unlock 1* course books,
teachers and learners will apply a multi-syllabi approach to provide a
standard to achieve the competencies specified in the Common
European Framework of Reference (CEFR) at level A1. Modern
English language teaching syllabi designs shift responsibility onto the
learner, and are an integrated product of two or more types. In multi-
dimensional syllabi, which is the approach to be utilized with the
Unlock 1 course books, there`s flexibility and more response to
variegation among students` needs. The students are on a training
course designed to prepare them for use of English in their vocation;
engineering. They will learn basic English before an exam based
selection process allowing the college at which they`re enrolled to
assess their ability and capacity to go further (A2) on their chosen

program of study.

Context

It's of use to review the types of syllabi that the multi-dimensional approach seeks to incorporate. In Stern's (1992) 'cultural syllabus', for example, the premise is language related to the situational context in which it occurs. Designers predict situations the learners find themselves in, and utilize these; for example, the British Council's 'going to the cinema' LearnEnglish Teens' listening exercise in which pictures are presented from movie genres, and the students are asked to complete a tick-box exercise to determine whether they think the picture is from a horror, science fiction, romance, comedy, action, historical drama, or cartoon film. In culturally based situations language is used and learned, so elements of the 'cultural syllabus' are important for the multi-approach. In skills' based syllabi, linguistic competencies (pronunciation, vocabulary, grammar, and discourse) merge to improve listening, writing, speaking, and reading, which is also useful in a multi-approach; as are grammar based elements of the formal syllabi in which the learner utilizes sequenced pattern practice drills focused on product. Task-based syllabi encourage communication to achieve purpose, so communicative methods can be employed by the multi-approach also. In task-based syllabi, learners focus on solving meaning. Speaking is through interactive practice and tasks relate to real needs. Process syllabi take shape, according to Breen (1984a:1984b), along with teaching and learning, and there're ongoing relations between subject matter, learning, and classroom contribution, which the multi-approach can adapt and benefit from. Breen and Candlin (1984) propose learner- led syllabi, where involvement increases motivation. However, pre- packed syllabi do provide support and guidance for instructors, who feel that the absence of a course book results in a lack of direction. Consequently, a hybrid of learner-led and pre-packed content is indicated in the constructing of the multi-approach. Proportional syllabi practically focus on spiraling techniques in which unit themes play a linking part, and lead to language recycling, which develops competence; as formal structure allied to theme becomes interactional.

In proportional syllabi, the focus is on what will be taught, rather than learned, which the multi-approach can utilize in its usage of the themes of the *Unlock 1* course books, that is, People, Seasons, Lifestyle, Places, Sport, Jobs, Homes and Buildings, Food and Culture, the Animal Kingdom, and Transport. Content-based syllabi teach specific information using learners` current language level; for example, in an engineering class. In an English for Special Purposes (ESP) setting, such as that of the engineers studying *Unlock 1*, specific informational content to do with engineering can be used to supplement the multi-approach, which will be the responsibility of the teachers in discussion with the students to establish their needs and provide appropriate supplementary material. With notional-functional syllabi, needs analysis is central to objectives, and so is utilizable by the multi-approach for the engineers` syllabus. The emphasis is communicative purpose, and conceptual meaning, that is, content as a number of functions performed; for example, inviting, requesting, agreeing, and apologizing. Ideally, notions are simultaneously expressed, for example, age, color, size, comparison, time, etc. Willis (1990, 129-130) believes lexical syllabi afford identification of common meaning to provide a typical pattern of English usage. Students reference their language learning to give them knowledge - after the fashion of an encyclopedia - to make valid and relevant generalizations. The multi-approach can adapt this in the form of note-taking, etc., to create an individual data base for each student to utilize suited to their learning needs.

The Content of the Syllabus: Academic Intensive English Program (IEP) plan

The curriculum for academic achievement will be determined by a standardized test to assess global competencies (Appendix 1) with illustrative descriptors to be found here - https://rm.coe.int/CoERMPublicCommonSearchServices/DisplayDCTMContent?documentId=090000168045bc7b. To help monitor and ensure standards, teachers should produce lesson plans containing objectives, outcomes, and success criteria. A basic outline of lesson differentiation, clear basic transitions, formative assessment, and students` activity based engagements should also be included. Daily lessons (see Appendix 2) to consist of, in Period 1, Reading and Writing, and Period 2, Listening and Speaking. In Period 3 the students will engage in Reading and Writing Practice and/or Listening and Speaking Practice.

Methodology

Unlock 1 by Cambridge University Press is the course text at level A1

(see Appendix 3). All the material in the textbooks should be covered

using the methodological tools given in the course descriptor (pp. 4-7):

choral speaking; class discussion conducted by teacher; construction of

vocabulary lists; crossword/word search puzzles; demonstrations by

teacher; notebook; open textbook study; oral questions by teacher

answered orally by students; photographs; reading aloud; reading

assignments; role playing; small groups` task oriented discussion, etc.,

supervised study during class period; textbook assignments; units of

instruction organized by topics; use of multimedia; use of recordings;

use of whiteboard (by instructor and students) vocabulary drills, and

word association activities. Teachers should familiarize themselves

with the global competencies required by the CEFR and supplement

the `scaffolding` content of the textbook, which shouldn`t be viewed as

providing global coverage of the CEFR standards. *Unlock* comes with an associated Learning Management System

(https://www.cambridgelms.org/main/p/splash), which teachers should

utilize, along with the e-learning component. Krashen`s (1982)

`Monitor theory` will be of some value, that is, subconscious acquisition

processes as more important than conscious learning (Stern, p. 80),

which is important for students` self-preparedness in the e-program. In

short, there should be some reliance from the teacher upon subconscious

acquisition of language in L2 learning in the students` progress, which

will likely be manifest in the e-learning computer based element of the

program when each individual student is alone with their tasks.

Assessment will be formative and summative. At the end of the course,

there`ll be a standardized English language proficiency test. At weeks 3,

6 and 9 there`ll be achievement tests to assess progress (not

proficiency), and based on the content of the textbook. Instructors

should use their knowledge, skills and experience to deliver a learning

program with clear articulation of lesson objectives, outcomes, and

success criteria.

The program should promote active learning through activity led learning with clear transitions between lesson aspects, and stress on the communicative competence of learners to focus on skills that supplement knowledge, while emphasizing formative assessment. Questioning strategies will focus on questions stimulative of higher order thinking skills and BRT will be integrated in all learning activities.

Conclusion

As approaches where learners are actively engaged in the classroom

encourage learning, Communicative Language Teaching, CLT, and

similar alternative methodologies are recommended. Students need to

be engaged in peer-peer interaction through group work, so the teacher

needs to be a facilitator more than a lecturer.

Appendix 1

CEFR Global Descriptors

A2 Understands sentences and common expressions related to

reasons of most immediate relevance (e.g. basic personal and family

information, shopping, local geography, employment). Communicates

on simple/routine tasks requiring simple/direct exchange of

information on familiar/ routine matters. Describes in simple terms

aspects of his/her background, immediate environment, and matters in

areas of immediate need.

A1 Understands and uses familiar every day expressions, and very basic phrases aimed at the satisfaction of needs of a concrete type. Can introduce him/herself and others, and can ask/answer questions about personal details; such as where he/she lives, people he/she knows, and things he/she has. Interacts in a simple way; provided the other person talks slowly and clearly, and is prepared to help.

Appendix 2

Program guidelines: 10 weeks plus 2 weeks e-learning

Daily Schedule: 3 classes per day, 100 minutes: Period 1, 2, and 120 minutes Period 3. Class Schedule: 8:00 am - 9:40 am. Period 1 9:40 am - 10:00 am (break); 10:00 am - 11:40 am. Period 2 11:40 am - 12:00 pm (break); 12:00 pm - 01:00 pm. Period 3-A 01:00 pm - 01:30 pm (lunch); 01:30 pm - 02:30 pm. Period 3-B 02:30 pm (finish). Late Policy: After 10 minutes, by the teachers' watch, the students is counted late for that period.

Absence Policy: Students aren`t allowed to be absent for more than 4 successive classes (8 hrs). Otherwise, their grade may be affected. Excused absences won`t affect grades or assessments.

Program grades; given by teachers:

10 % In- class Proficiency

40 % Results of the progress tests

15 % Quizzes

10 % Preparedness and Participation

10 % Attendance

15% for e-learning (through Rosetta Stone Language Learning

software, https://www.rosettastone.com/)

Semester Schedule:

10 weeks (2 terms, 5 weeks each)

Semester Begins

Week 3 First Progress Test

Mid-semester Break

Week 6   Second Progress Test

Week 9 Third Progress Test

Week 10 Exam

Semester Ends

Week 11 and 12 e-learning

Appendix 3

A1 to A2 Syllabus

Teacher:	Institution:	Location:	Program Title and Level: General English
	Books: *Unlock* 1 - *Reading & Writing*, and *Listening & Speaking*	Date:	Session Duration:100 minutes Period 1 and 2 and 120 minutes Period 3

Week 1	Grammar	Choral	Reading	Formative Assessment	Videos
Topic: People	Nouns and verbs; singular and plural nouns; the verb *be* Personal pronouns; possessive determiners; possessive adjectives Lexis; family vocabulary (e.g. grandfather, grandmother, father, mother, etc.) Jobs, countries and nationalities	Speaking; class discussion; conducted by teacher Construction of vocab lists Crossword/ wordsearch puzzles Demonstration by teacher; notebook Open text book study Oral questions by teacher; answered orally by students Photographs Reading aloud Reading	Previewing; understanding key vocabulary Skimming; scanning to find information Writing; punctuation Write descriptive sentences about somebody in your family Listening Understanding key vocabulary Listening; for main ideas (gist);	Unit 1 spelling test Unit 1 Q & A Discussion Written Work Observation Peer correction Verbal feedback	People: the film makers

Week 1	Grammar	Choral	Reading	Formative Assessment	Videos
		Role Playing Small groups; such as task oriented discussion Supervised study during class period Textbook assignments Units of instruction organized by topics Use of multimedia Use of recordings Use of whiteboard (by instructor and students)	Syllable stress Speaking Introducing and starting a talk; saying words and sentences in syllables; students tell the group about two famous people from their country		

Week 1	Grammar	Choral	Reading	Formative Assessment	Videos
		Vocabulary drills Word association activity			

End of Unit 1 Test - *Unlock* Teachers Book 1 R & W pp. 99-101 *Unlock* 1 S & L pp. 106-107.

Week 2	Grammar	Reading	Formative Assessment	Videos
Topic: Seasons	Adjectives and nouns Noun phrases; Subject and verb Prepositions Prepositional phrases *There is* and *there are* Lexis Adjectives to describe the weather (e.g. warm, hot, cold, sunny) Months and seasons Weather Colors	Scanning to find information Previewing Understanding key vocabulary Writing Punctuation: capital letters Write facts about the weather in their city Listening Use visuals to predict content Understand key vocabulary Listen for main ideas	Unit 2 spelling test Unit 2 test Q & A Discussion Written Work Observation Peer correction Verbal feedback	Extreme weather; Seasons in North America

Week 2 Grammar   Reading   Formative   Videos
                                       Assessment

                      (gist) Listen

                      for detail

                      Sentence stress

                      Speaking

                      Describe

                      photographs

                      Word stress

                      Describe

                      photographs of

                      a landscape

End of Unit 2 Test - *Unlock* Teachers Book 1 R & W pp. 102-104 *Unlock* 1

S & L pp. 108-109.

Week 3	Grammar	Reading	Formative Assessment	Videos
Topic: Lifestyle	Collocation Subject-verb-object Present simple Time expressions Lexis Vocabulary for study (subjects, i.e., Math, History, Chemistry, Business) Days of the week Time expressions Collocation for lifestyle	Scan to find information Preview Understand key vocabulary Writing Spelling third person singular forms Write facts; about the lifestyle of a student in their class Listening Listen for main ideas (gist) Listen for	Unit 3 spelling test Unit 3 test Q & A Discussion Written Work Observation Peer correction Verbal feedback	Life under ground: The Bedouin

Week 3	Grammar	Reading	Formative Assessment	Videos
	lifestyle, (e.g. download apps, go to the gym, have dinner with friends)	detail Understand key vocabulary Intonation Speaking Asking and answering Intonation in questions Interview students for a survey		

End of Unit 3 Test - *Unlock* Teachers Book 1 R & W pp. 105-107 *Unlock* 1 S & L pp. 110-111.

Progress Test 1.

Week 4	Grammar	Reading	Formative Assessment	Videos
Topic: Places	Noun phrases with *of*	Read for main ideas (gist)	Unit 4 spelling test	France: The Great Barrier Reef
	There is/ there are	Read for detail	Unit 4 test	
	Determiners; articles	Understand key vocabulary	Q & A	
	The imperative	Preview	Discussion	
	Prepositions of place	Scan to find information	Written work	
	Lexis Vocabulary for places in a city (e.g. museum, library, factory, monument)	Writing	Observation	
	Vocabulary for places in the	Spelling and punctuation: capital letters	Peer correction	
		Write facts about their country	Verbal feedback	
		Listening		
		Listen for main ideas		

Week 4	Grammar	Reading	Formative Assessment	Videos
	country (e.g. hill, farm, field, forest) Vocabulary for places (e.g. bank, bridge, library, mosque) Prepositions of place	(gist) Listen for detail Understand key vocabulary Intonation Speaking Ask for and give directions Pronounce phrases		

End of Unit 4 Test - *Unlock* Teachers Book 1 R & W - pp. 108-110 *Unlock* 1 S & L pp. 112-113.

Week 5	Grammar	Reading	Formative Assessment	Videos
Topic: Sport	Sports collocation preposition Adjectives Subject-verb-adjective Subject-verb-adverb Comparing adjectives Lexis Adjectives to describe sports (e.g. hard, exciting, expensive, difficult) Vocabulary for sport	Use knowledge to predict content Understand key vocabulary Read for main ideas (gist) Read for detail Scan to find information Scan to predict content Writing Punctuation: commas Write facts	Unit 5 spelling test Unit 5 test Q & A Discussion Written work Observation Peer correction Verbal feedback	Tai-chi and Shaolin Kung-Fu; Free diving

Week 5	Grammar	Reading	Formative Assessment	Videos
	collocation (e.g. play tennis, go swimming, do karate)	about a popular sport in their country Listening Key vocabulary Listen for main ideas (gist) Listen for detail Speaking Compare and introduce a talk Weak vowel sounds		

Week 5   Grammar   Reading   Formative   Videos
                                  Assessment

Pronounce
clusters of
consonants
(e.g. - *gh*, -
ing, ph, ck)
Compare
different
kinds   of
sport   and
exercise

End of Unit 5 Test - *Unlock* Teachers Book 1 R & W - pp. 111-113
Unlock 1 S & L pp. 114-115.

Spring Break April 2 -6.

Week 6	Grammar	Reading	Formative Assessment	Videos
Topic: Jobs	Adjective phrases	Read for detail Preview	Unit 6 spelling test	Dabba-wallas
	Must and *have to*	Understand key	Unit 6 test	Fire rangers
	Joining sentences with *and*	vocabulary	Q & A	
		Scan to find	Discussion	
	Have/has to	information	Written work	
	Suffixes	Work out	Observation	
	Lexis	meaning from	Peer correction	
	Vocabulary	context	Verbal	
	for jobs (e.g.	Writing	feedback	
	vet, fireman,	Contractions		
	manages	Write		
	people,	sentences		
	prepares	Write a		
	food)	description of a		
	Adjectives	job for a friend		
	for people	Listening		
	(e.g. good-	Listen for		
	looking, kind,	opinion		
	polite, slim)	Predict content		
		Understand		

Week 6	Grammar	Reading	Formative Assessment	Videos
	Collocations for jobs, e.g., build houses, do experiments, serve food	key vocabulary Listen for main ideas (gist) Listen for detail Speaking; ask for and give reasons Pronounce consonants in have to, have, has to, has (e.g. /f/, /v/, /z/, /s/) Choose a person for a job		

End of Unit 6 Test - *Unlock* Teachers Book 1 R & W pp. 114-116
Unlock 1 S & L pp. 116-117.
Progress Test 2.

Week 7	Grammar	Reading	Formative Assessment	Videos
Topic: Homes and buildings	Comparing quantities Comparative adjectives Joining sentences with but (linking words) Should Lexis Vocabulary for buildings (e.g. cinema, library, hotel, train station) Vocabulary for parts of buildings (e.g. car park, stairs, exit, garden)	Use visuals to predict content Scan to find information Read for detail Preview Understand discourse Compare data Writing Spelling: double consonants Write a comparison Write a comparison of two buildings Listening Listen for	Unit 7 spelling test Unit 7 test Q & A Discussion Written work Observation Peer correction Verbal feedback	Building the new Shanghai Homes in Dharavi, India

Week 7	Grammar	Reading	Formative Assessment	Videos
	Adjectives to describe buildings (e.g. big, modern, old, ugly) Vocabulary for rooms (e.g. bedroom, bathroom, living room, kitchen) Adjectives for furniture (e.g. comfortable, wooden, glass)	reasons Understand key vocabulary Listen for main ideas (gist) Listen for detail Speaking; ask for and give opinions Agree and disagree Discuss ideas for a new building Linking		

End of Unit 7 Test - *Unlock* Teachers Book 1 R & W pp. 117-119 *Unlock 1*S & L
pp. 118-119.

Week 8	Grammar	Reading	Formative Assessment	Videos
Topic: Food and culture	Countable and uncountable nouns (some, any, much, many) Subject-verb agreement Determiners: a, an and some Lexis Vocabulary for food and drink (e.g. potatoes, coconut, yogurt, water)	words Skim Preview Understand key vocabulary Scan to find information Read for detail Writing Spelling Write descriptive sentences Write about food in their country for a student website Listening Listen for numbers Understand key vocabulary	Unit 8 spelling test Unit 8 test Q & A Discussion Written work Observation Peer correction Verbal feedback	Mexican food; Chinese food

Week 8	Grammar	Reading	Formative Assessment	Videos
		Predict content using visuals Listen for main ideas (gist) Listen for detail Listen for the sounds – teen and -ty Speaking Introduce a report Talk about their results Sentence stress: emphasis Report the results of a survey		

End of Unit 8 Test - *Unlock* Teachers Book 1 R & W pp. 120-122 *Unlock 1* S & L pp. 120-121.

Week 9	Grammar	Reading	Formative Assessment	Videos
Topic: The animal kingdom	Can and cannot Superlatives Definitions (e.g. a kind of, that means, is the name for) Lexis Vocabulary to describe facts about animals (e.g. long, high, weighs, habitat) Vocabulary for animals (e.g. harmless, endangered, deadliest, nocturnal)	Read for main ideas Read for detail Understand key vocabulary Skim and scan to find information Understand discourse Writing Analyze a table of facts Write a descriptive paragraph Write a paragraph about an animal Listening Listen for	Unit 9 spelling test Unit 9 test Q & A Discussion Written work Observation Peer correction Verbal feedback	South African wildlife; Animals and people

<table>
<tr><td>Week 9</td><td>Grammar</td><td>Reading</td><td>Formative
Assessment</td><td>Videos</td></tr>
<tr><td></td><td></td><td>definitions
Understand key words
Listen for main ideas (gist)
Listen for detail
Speaking
Introduce a topic
Use questions in a talk
Pronunciation: pauses
Describe an animal</td><td></td><td></td></tr>
</table>

End of Unit 9 Test - *Unlock* Teachers Book 1 R & W pp. 123-126 *Unlock 1* S & L pp. 122-123.

Progress Test 3.

Week 10	Grammar	Reading	Formative Assessment	Videos
Topic: Transport	Quantifiers Subject-verb-object Linking sentences with pronouns The past simple Lexis Vocabulary for transport; collocations (e.g. take the bus, travel by car) Describe a solution Describe results Describe a solution to a transport problem	Work out meaning from context Preview Skim and scan to find information Understand key vocabulary Read for detail Understand discourse Writing Collect data with a survey Take notes Error correction Write a paragraph about transport in their city Listening Take	Unit 10 spelling test Unit 10 test Q & A Discussion Written work Observation Peer correction Verbal feedback	Tokyo transport Alaskan transport

Week	Grammar	Reading	Formative Assessment	Videos
10		Notes Predict content using visuals Listen for main ideas (gist) Listen for detail Speaking Describe a topic; describe a problem; describe a solution; describe results; describe a solution to a transport problem Pronunciation: pronouncing years (e.g.		

Week	Grammar	Reading	Formative Assessment	Videos
10		1994, nineteen ninety-four) Pronunciation: past simple endings: /t/,/d/,/ d/		

End of Unit 10 Test - *Unlock* Teachers Book 1 R & W pp. 127-129

Unlock 1 S & L pp. 124-125.

End of Program Exam followed by 2 weeks of e-learning using the Rosetta Stone ELT software.

Bibliography

Breen, M.P. (1984a). Process Syllabuses for the Language Classroom. In Brumfit, C. J. (ed.) *General English Syllabus Design* Pergamon Press Ltd. and the British Council.

Breen, M.P. (1984b). Process in syllabus design and classroom language learning. In C.J. Brumfit (ed.). *General English Syllabus Design. ELT Docum*ents No. 118. London: Pergamon Press & The British Council.

British Council, LearnEnglish Teens, Listening Skills Practice: Going to the cinema - exercises, http://learnenglishteens.britishcouncil.org/sites/teens/files/going_to_the _cinema_-_exercises_3.pdf

Cambridge Placement Test, University of Cambridge ESOL Examinations, Cambridge, http://www.democpt.cambridgetest.org/cptApp/demoTest.html?method =languageSelection .

Cambridge English Language Assessment, Cambridge Learning

Management System (LMS), Cambridge University Press,

https://www.cambridgelms.org/main/p/splash .

Candlin, C.N.(1984). Applying a System Approach to Curriculum

Innovation in the Public Sector. In Read, J.A.S. (ed.) *Trends in*

Language Syllabus Design. Singapore: SEAMEO Regional

Language Center.

Krashen, S. (1982). *Principles and practice in second language*

acquisition. Oxford: Pergamon Press.

Mohseni Far M.A., Mohammad (January, 2008). Shahid Chamran

University, Iran. An Overview of Syllabuses in English Language

Teaching. In *Karen's Linguistics Issues.*

Ostrowska, Sabina *Unlock 1 Reading and Writing*, Cambridge

University Press, 2014.

Stern, Hans Heinrich (1992). Language teaching objectives. In P.

Allen and B. Harley (eds.) *Issues and Options in Language*

Teaching (pp 63- 99). Oxford: Oxford University Press.

White, N. M. *Unlock 1 Listening and Speaking*, Cambridge University Press, 2014.

Willis, D. (1990). *The Lexical Syllabus: A New Approach to Language Teaching*. London: COBUILD.

* All images were free to adapt and use commercially.

I want morebooks!

Buy your books fast and straightforward online - at one of world's fastest growing online book stores! Environmentally sound due to Print-on-Demand technologies.

Buy your books online at
www.morebooks.shop

Kaufen Sie Ihre Bücher schnell und unkompliziert online – auf einer der am schnellsten wachsenden Buchhandelsplattformen weltweit! Dank Print-On-Demand umwelt- und ressourcenschonend produziert.

Bücher schneller online kaufen
www.morebooks.shop

KS OmniScriptum Publishing
Brivibas gatve 197
LV-1039 Riga, Latvia
Telefax: +371 686 204 55

info@omniscriptum.com
www.omniscriptum.com

Printed by Books on Demand GmbH, Norderstedt / Germany